Basketball

Clive Gifford

W

FRANKLIN WATTS

LONDON • SYDNEY

This edition 2011

Franklin Watts
338 Euston Road
London NW1 3BH

Franklin Watts Australia
Level 17/207 Kent Street
Sydney NSW 2000

© Franklin Watts 2008, 2011
Series editor: Jeremy Smith
Art director: Jonathan Hair

Series designed and created for Franklin Watts by Painted Fish Ltd.
Designer: Rita Storey
Editor: Nicola Edwards
Photography: Tudor Photography, Banbury

A CIP catalogue record for this book is available from the British Library.

Dewey classification: 796.323
ISBN: 978 1 4451 0139 2
Printed in China

Franklin Watts is a division of Hachette Children's Books, an Hachette UK company. www.hachette.co.uk

Note: At the time of going to press for this paperback edition, the statistics and player profiles in this book were up to date. However, due to some players' active participation in the sport, it is possible that some of these may now be out of date.

This paperback edition has been fully revised and updated.

Picture credits
© Peter Casolino/Alamy p13b,
© Aflo Foto Agency/Alamy p19b,
© Reuters/Corbis p6, 21, © John Kolesidis/Reuters/Corbis p7, © Larry W. Smith/epa/Corbis p19 and 25.
Cover images: Tudor Photography, Banbury.

All photos posed by models.
Thanks to Daniel Browne, Leanne Ong, Owen and Christian Seeney.

The Publisher would like to thank Blessed George Napier Catholic School for the use of their sport facilities and coach James Sturla for his assistance.

Taking part in sport is a fun way to get fit, but like any form of physical exercise it has an element of risk, particularly if you are unfit, overweight or suffer from any medical conditions. It is advisable to consult a healthcare professional before beginning any programme of exercise.

Contents

What is Basketball?

Basketball is a fast and dynamic team ball sport. It is played by five players a side with rolling substitutions. This means that players on the bench – up to five or seven depending on the competition – can swap places with a player on the court and join in a game at any time.

Scoring Points

Basketball is played on a rectangular court. At each end stands a hoop 3.05 metres off the ground, usually with a rectangular panel called a backboard behind it. The players in the attacking team move the ball around by passing and catching it or by bouncing the ball as they run, which is called dribbling. The aim is to get into a position to shoot at the hoop. A successful shot, known as a basket, is worth two points. Three points can be scored for a longer range shot which has to be taken outside of the three point line marked on the court (see page 8).

The players in the opposing team aim to stop baskets being scored and try to gain possession of the ball themselves. If either side makes a foul (see page 11), the officials refereeing the game can award free throws to the fouled side. Each of these throws, if a basket is scored as a result, adds one point to a team's score.

Top Competitions

Apart from the Olympics, the basketball world is split into two camps. Most of the world plays under rules set by FIBA, which organizes the World Championships for men and women as well as the Euroleague for Europe's top clubs and the European Championship for the continent's best national teams. In America and under its own, slightly different rules, the National Basketball Association (NBA) was formed in 1949

Shaquille O'Neal performs a slam dunk. He gets his hand above the basket and slams the ball in from above.

and has grown to become the most glamorous competition in the sport. A women's version, the WNBA, was formed in 1997.

Basketball for All

Basketball is a sport that people of different abilities can play and enjoy. Games can vary from an informal gathering with friends in a park to competitive matches in clubs and leagues. For younger players, there are scaled down versions of the game. Mini basketball is amongst the most popular and is played by teams of five children with a smaller ball and simpler rules. Wheelchair-bound players have their own fast-moving and action-filled version of the game. Wheelchair basketball is booming in popularity and is one of the most-watched sports for elite athletes with a disability.

Basketball's History

Many team sports have developed gradually over hundreds of years. Basketball is different. In 1891 James Naismith, a Canadian PE instructor working in America, invented the sport to keep students fit during winter, using a soccer ball and court marked out in a gymnasium. Basketball's popularity grew quickly in colleges in the United States and spread to other countries. The sport entered the Olympics in 1936, four years after the International Basketball Federation (FIBA) was formed, although at first only men could compete. It was another 40 years before the women's game was admitted.

In the Beginning

James Naismith's original game of "Basket Ball" used peach baskets without a hole in the bottom. Someone used to have to grab a ladder and retrieve the ball after every score!

Two wheelchair basketball players contest a high ball during a 2004 Paralympics match between France and Australia.

This player makes a short range shot. If successful, his side will score two points.

A basketball court is 28m long by 15m wide under FIBA rules (28.65m x 15.24m in the NBA). Indoor courts are usually made of wood and sprung to make them flexible underfoot. At each end is a 45cm-wide hoop fitted with a net and with a backboard behind it.

On the Court

The court is divided into two halves. The half in which a team is attacking is called the front court and the other half, the back court. Once the players in a team have the ball in their back

court, they must cross the halfway line within eight seconds or possession goes to the other team. They cannot return to their back court without losing possession either.

Play continues until the officials signal a foul or violation (see page 11), there is some other stoppage or the ball goes out of the court. A player holding the ball who steps on the sideline or the end lines also takes the ball out of the court. When the ball goes out of the court, a player from the team that didn't touch it last restarts play by throwing the ball in from the sideline or end line.

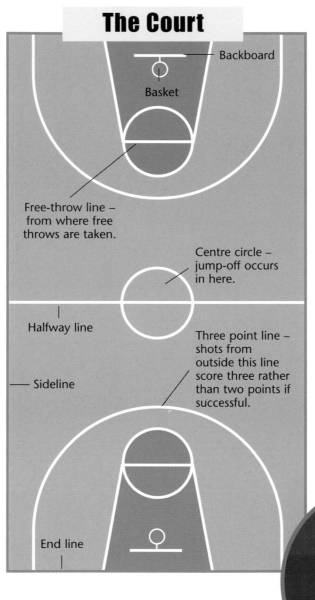

The Court

Backboard

Basket

Free-throw line – from where free throws are taken.

Centre circle – jump-off occurs in here.

Halfway line

Three point line – shots from outside this line score three rather than two points if successful.

Sideline

End line

 The key – attackers can only stay in this area for a maximum of three seconds.

A basketball is an air-filled ball covered in leather or a synthetic material with a pimpled or pebbled outer surface to aid grip. It should have a circumference of between 75 and 78 cm.

When the ball goes out over one of the sidelines, a player from the team that didn't touch it last receives the ball and restarts the game with a sideline throw. The player taking the throw must pass the ball to a team-mate within five seconds.

Footwear and Preparation

With so much running, jumping, twisting and turning in basketball, players have to pay great attention to their footwear and their game preparation. Basketball boots may be cut quite high to offer plenty of ankle support, or cut a little lower. In either case, they should fit very well and be comfortable, with plenty of cushioning inside.

Clothing and Equipment

Basketball players mustn't wear jewellery or watches and what they do wear needs to be carefully considered. For casual games, cotton T-shirts and shorts or a sports skirt are fine, but in competition players tend to wear specialist nylon basketball kit which is lightweight and comfortable. Many players wear a sweatband or headband to help mop up sweat as well as leaving a towel on the sidelines. A tracksuit to keep warm before and after the game and water bottle to take small sips from during breaks in play are also essential items.

Warming up

Warming up and stretching muscles is essential in such an athletic sport. All players must put a lot of effort into warming up well and stretching all their muscles so that they are in the best possible condition to take part in a game.

Two players, one from each team, contest a jump ball in the centre circle, trying to tip it towards one of their team-mates. Jump balls, also known as jump-offs or tip-offs, are used to start a basketball game when the referee throws the ball into the air.

A basketball game is run by a set of officials, the most important of which are the umpire and the referee. They stand on opposite sides of the court and judge on rules, successful shots, whether the ball is in or out of play and on any fouls and violations that occur. In the case of a dispute, the referee is in overall charge.

Game Time

NBA games are made up of four 12-minute quarters, whilst FIBA games are split into four 10-minute quarters. Other durations are sometimes used in college and school basketball. In many competitions, if the scores are tied at the end of the game, a five minute period of overtime is played to determine the winner. If the scores are still drawn at the end of overtime, another overtime period can be played and so on.

Stop the Clock

Whenever the referee blows the whistle the game stops and so does the game clock, which is controlled by an official. The clock only restarts once the ball is back in play, touched by a player on court or after the last free throw (see page 11) is taken. A free throw is an unchallenged shot from in front of the basket and is worth one point. Time-outs are a short, usually one or two minute, break in play called by one team's coach (in the NBA, a player can also call a time-out). Each team has a maximum number of

Foul

Jump ball

Holding

Two points scored

Travelling

Blocking

The referee and umpire use their whistles and hand signals to communicate their decision to players, coaches, other officials and spectators. Here are some of the most common signals.

time-outs in a game. The number varies depending on the competition.

Fouls

Basketball is supposed to be a non-contact sport, although watching a top game from the Olympics, Euroleague or NBA, it can sometimes appear anything but. The officials have to judge whether the contact is enough to signal a foul. Many fouls in basketball are defensive fouls, those committed by the defender. These include pushing, tripping, holding, striking or blocking an opponent from moving on the court. Offensive fouls include charging (see page 21). A player who performs a foul has it awarded against

This player is taking a free throw. Players who are fouled as they shoot are awarded free throws. All other players must stay outside of the key until the last free throw in a series is taken.

them by the officials who also award between one and three free throws to the other team. Players who collect five personal fouls are 'benched' – they have to leave the court and cannot take any further part in that game.

Violations

A violation occurs when the player breaks a rule of the game. It is not as serious as a foul and usually results in the officials awarding the ball to the other team. Common violations include travelling (see page 13), retreating into your own back court with the ball and performing either a carry or double dribble (see page 16). A number of violations are connected with time rules. For example, a team gaining possession of the ball on court has a maximum of 24 seconds in which to make a shot.

A Foul Record

During the 1983-84 season, Darryl Dawkins recorded the most ever personal fouls in an NBA season, a record 386!

The defender (right) is fouling his opponent with the ball by pulling his shirt and holding him back.

Receiving and Pivoting

Bringing the ball under control is a priority in basketball. Once players have the ball under control and in their hands, they have five seconds to release it in the form of a dribble, shot or pass. If they dawdle, the officials may signal a violation and give the ball to the other team.

Receiving the Ball

Before players can pass the ball, they have to receive it. This usually involves catching it, ideally with two hands and bringing it in securely to the body to protect the ball from opponents. Ideal catching height is between the waist and chest, but players learn to be alert for a ball coming towards them at all heights and angles. To receive a ball well, players get into a balanced position to catch the ball and watch it into their hands. They aim to meet the ball with their arms and hands relaxed, ready to cushion the ball's impact.

The Triple Threat Stance

When a player receives the ball, he or she should look to get into the triple threat stance as quickly as possible. This posture, with the head up and the ball in a position to be moved, allows a player to move quickly into a dribble, make a pass or attempt a shot. When marked closely, a player in this stance may fake to do one thing such as a low pass only to do something else instead, such as jump and shoot.

The Triple Threat Stance

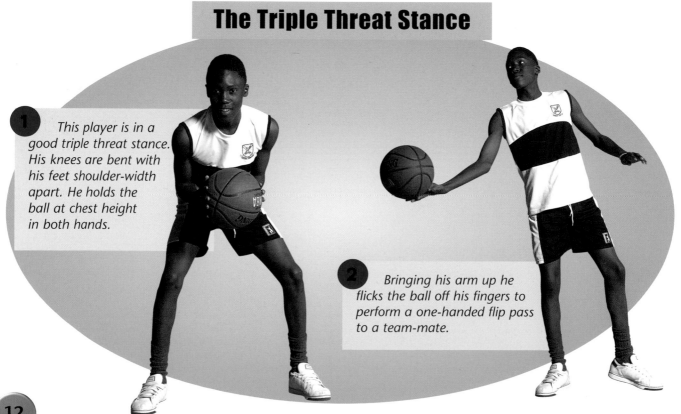

1. This player is in a good triple threat stance. His knees are bent with his feet shoulder-width apart. He holds the ball at chest height in both hands.

2. Bringing his arm up he flicks the ball off his fingers to perform a one-handed flip pass to a team-mate.

Pivoting

1 *This player receives the ball and decides to turn. He stays on the ball of his left foot which acts as a pivot as he lifts up his other foot.*

2 *Twisting on the ball of his pivot foot, he turns, taking small steps with his right foot. His head is up and looking around, searching out his next move.*

3 *Completing his pivoting, he decides to play an overhead pass. He raises his arms and snaps his wrists and fingers forward to send the ball to its target.*

Travelling and Pivoting

When catching the ball, a player must stop moving within two steps or a violation called travelling will be called and the ball handed over to the opposing team. Players can, however, keep one foot planted on the floor and turn and step round with their other foot. This is called pivoting and is a vital skill as it allows the player to change direction to seek out a pass or turn towards the basket for a shot. Players try to stay on the balls of their feet so that their pivoting movement is smooth and quick. They can take as many steps as they like with their non-pivot foot as long as their pivot foot doesn't move.

Diana Taurasi (right) battles for a rebound with Kara Lawson during a game in the women's basketball championships.

Diana Taurasi

Date of birth: June 11th, 1982

Nationality: American

Height: 1.83m

Weight: 78kg

Diana plays for Phoenix Mercury. She has league scoring records for scoring average (25.3), points in a season (860), and shares single-game record (47). Her other achievements include:

• WNBA Rookie of the Year 2004

• WNBA Most valuable player of the year in 2009

Member of the USA national basketball team:

• 2008 Olympics: Gold

• 2006 World Championship: Bronze

• 2004 Olympics: Gold

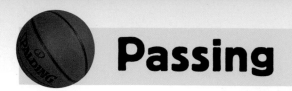

Passing

Players can move the ball faster around the court by passing it to team-mates than they can through dribbling the ball. Good passing can get a side out of trouble, break through defences and lead to plenty of baskets being scored. It is such a crucial set of skills that it should be practised whenever possible.

Passing Practice

Some passes can be practised solo using a wall to bounce the ball against for chest passes or as a guide to sending the ball at the right height for a bounce pass. Passing practice, though, is best done with one or more team-mates. Practise receiving the ball, pivoting and then passing. Practise making cuts (short sprints into space) and being ready to receive the ball. Games and drills played in small squares such as two

The Chest Pass

1 The player holds the ball around its back with his wrists bent back and thumbs behind the ball.

2 He pushes his arms out firmly, moving his body forward in the direction of the pass. As his arms straighten, he flicks his wrists forward to release the ball. The ball travels almost flat towards the receiver. The passer's hands should end up pointing in the direction of the ball's path.

3 The receiver keeps her eyes on the ball all the way into her hands. She receives the ball in both hands with her fingers spread around the ball. She keeps her wrists and arms loose to help cushion the ball's pace and prevent a dropped catch.

The One-Handed Bounce Pass

1 *Seeing a receiver free, the passer steps sharply to the side on which he wishes to make the pass. He keeps his pivot foot planted and both hands on the ball.*

2 *Leaning to the side, he releases his non-throwing hand from the ball and drives the ball forward and down. He aims for a point past the defender and around two-thirds of the way to the receiver.*

3 *The ball bounces past the defender and the receiver moves to collect the ball. A well-executed one-handed bounce pass should result in the ball being caught by the receiver at around waist height.*

passers versus one defender or three versus two can help sharpen your passing and movement skills.

A choice of Passes

Used over short and medium distances, the chest pass (see page 14) is the most common pass in basketball.

If a defender is standing relatively close and blocking off a chest pass, a bounce pass can be a good option. This can be performed with two hands, or, as shown above, with one hand. The one-handed bounce pass is a little trickier to perfect but it does allow you

to lean and send the ball further away from an opponent.

Passing Pointers

When making any pass, the passer and receiver must establish contact before the pass is made. Possession can often be lost when the receiver isn't ready or is looking away not expecting a pass. A good pass not only avoids being intercepted by the other team, it also sends the ball to the receiver at the right speed, height and position to be caught. Choosing the exact moment to pass and how much force you put on the ball can be vital.

Dribbling

Dribbling is moving around whilst bouncing the ball up and down with one hand. Dribbling allows a single player to move round the court, but it is a skill that needs concentration and rhythm as players pump the ball up and down. Learning to dribble equally well with both hands doubles the potential impact you can make on a game.

Dribbling Rules

You are allowed to swap hands in the middle of a dribble but if you catch the ball in both hands and start dribbling again, you perform a double dribble. A double dribble is a violation and results in possession passing to the opposing team. Another violation to avoid is the carry. This is where you twist your dribbling hand past 90 degrees to cradle the ball. A dribble has to end in a pass or a shot. Sometimes, a player is able to dribble and drive hard to the

The Basic Dribble

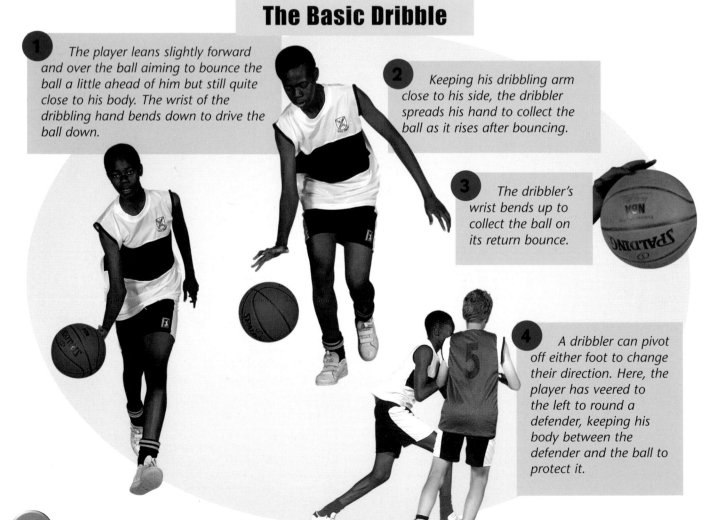

1 The player leans slightly forward and over the ball aiming to bounce the ball a little ahead of him but still quite close to his body. The wrist of the dribbling hand bends down to drive the ball down.

2 Keeping his dribbling arm close to his side, the dribbler spreads his hand to collect the ball as it rises after bouncing.

3 The dribbler's wrist bends up to collect the ball on its return bounce.

4 A dribbler can pivot off either foot to change their direction. Here, the player has veered to the left to round a defender, keeping his body between the defender and the ball to protect it.

The Speed Dribble

1 To perform the faster speed dribble, the dribbler angles his hand a little to push the ball down further ahead of him so that he can run onto it.

2 The dribbler pushes the ball down with more force so that it will bounce higher than in a regular dribble.

3 The speed dribble can sometimes be used to sprint past defenders to make a fast break down the court towards the opponent's basket.

basket to perform a lay-up (see pages 20–21). On other occasions, their path may be blocked and they may stop dribbling to pivot and look for a pass.

The Basic Dribble
The basic dribble is quite low, usually between knee and waist height. Bouncing the ball higher than that can make the ball easier for an opponent to steal. You can protect your dribble by positioning your body between the ball and an opponent as

you dribble. Practice will enable you to dribble by touch alone, allowing you to keep your head up to scan the game ahead. Good dribblers are able to dribble with both hands and perform dribbles at different heights and speeds, often with tricks to deceive opponents.

The Speed Dribble
A higher, faster dribble can be made to move at speed down the court, particularly when one team makes a fast break out of its own half.

Attacking

Whenever players in a team get the ball, they go on the attack. They look to get close to the opponents' basket and through dribbling, passing and intelligent movement try to get one of their team-mates into the best possible position to take a shot at the basket.

Slow and Fast

Some attacks happen very fast, such as when a player intercepts a loose pass and sprints to the basket. Others can take longer and involve a number of passes and dribbles. Attackers should keep the ball moving and aim to draw defenders out of position whilst looking for a way to get close to the basket.

Finding and Using Space

Attackers support their team-mate who has the ball by getting into space. They use skills such as changes of pace and switches in direction to cut away from and get free of a defender who is marking them. Other players can create space for their team-mates to move into by making a run away

The Give and Go

1 *The player (left) makes a chest pass to a team-mate. As soon as the ball leaves her hands, she sprints forward. The receiver leans to collect the ball.*

2 *The receiver catches the ball and pivots to his left before passing the ball back to the original passer. In the process, the defender in blue has been cut out of the play by the two passes.*

from the space, hoping to draw their defender with them. Using space well is especially important in the key (see page 8), where a player is only allowed to stand for three seconds.

Give and Go

There are many team attacking moves which can be practised by players watched by their coach. One of the simplest is the 'give and go' (see page 8), a pair of passes between two team-mates that cuts out a defender.

Fake Plays

There are many different fakes that attackers can perform to trick an opponent into thinking they will do one thing when they end up doing something else. For the player with the ball, faking a low pass can cause the defender to lunge low, leaving the attacker free to make a quick overhead pass. An alternative move is to catch the ball then fake a pass to one side before driving forward and dribbling to the other side.

LeBron James in the 2008 Olympic Games Men's Basketball Final match between the United States and Spain.

LeBron James

Date of Birth: December 30th, 1984

Nationality: American

Height: 2.03m

Weight: 113kg

Nicknamed 'King James' he is listed as one of the highest paid sportsmen in the world. He plays for Cleveland Cavaliers.

• NBA Rookie of the Year 2004

• NBA Scoring Champion of the year in 2008

• NBA Most valuable player of the year in 2009

Member of the USA national basketball team:

• 2008 Olympics: Gold

• 2006 World Championship: Bronze

• 2004 Olympics: Bronze

The Lay-up

The lay-up is a type of driving move to the basket which ends with a scoring attempt. It is a vital play in all levels of basketball as it enables a player to get as close as possible to the basket for a shot. A lay-up can be made from either the left or the right side of the basket. The shot is made using the arm furthest from the centre of the court – so for example, if you are approaching the basket from the right, use your right arm.

Lay-up Skills
The lay-up requires just the right amount of force in releasing the ball so that it bounces off the backboard and into the hoop. Players tend to aim to bounce the ball off one of the top corners of the box marking on the backboard. Don't expect your first attempts

The Lay-up

1 The player may have been dribbling the ball beforehand or caught a pass whilst moving forwards. Once the ball is in both hands, each foot can only touch the floor once. The player takes a long, bouncy stride towards the basket.

2 As he lands on his jumping foot, the player flexes his knee and pushes hard off his jumping foot. His non-jumping leg bends at the knee and hurdles upwards. The player springs upwards with the ball raised but still in both his hands.

3 As the player rises, he stretches his body and arms upwards. Keeping his eyes on the basket, the player aims to release the ball with his fingertips at the highest point of their jump.

at lay-ups to end in success. Only practice will perfect both the rhythm needed in the steps to the basket and the accuracy of the shot. In a game, a lay-up is rarely uncontested. Players will find one or more defenders around them as they head for the basket. Under pressure, they must concentrate on their lay-up and focus on their target.

Players making a lay-up must be careful not to run or charge into a defender on their way to the basket. If defenders are set with both feet grounded before the attacker pushes into them, then the officials are likely to signal a charging foul against the attacker.

Michael Jordan springs up at the end of a lay-up to score a basket.

4. With his palm facing the backboard, the player pushes the ball to bounce off the backboard and through the hoop. The player continues to watch the ball as he lands in case a basket isn't scored. He may be able to jump or stretch to retrieve the ball from the rebound.

Michael Jordan

Date of Birth: February 17th, 1963

Nationality: American

Height: 1.98m

Weight: 98kg

Michael Jordan is the most famous name in basketball. His explosive shooting, incredible jumping and agility in the air and brilliant all-round game propelled the Chicago Bulls to six NBA titles. Jordan won two Olympic gold medals, the first in 1984 as a college amateur and the second in 1992 as a member of the professional US Dream Team. He had a spell playing baseball for the Chicago White Sox and also came out of retirement for a second time to lead the Washington Wizards. Jordan holds many NBA records including its highest ever career scoring average – he scored an average of 30.1 points per game and amassed 32,292 NBA points in total.

Shooting

The lay-up is just one type of shot players can make. Others include the jump shot and the set shot. The set shot is used for taking free throws after a foul and also when a player is close to the basket.

The Set Shot

The set shot starts with the ball brought up to around head height so that from the front it covers one half of your face. The player's feet should be shoulder-width apart and both your feet and shoulders should point towards the basket.

Shooting Success

The secret of good shooting is to practise regularly and often so that you perfect your shooting action. With time, you will get used to how much force and what angle you need to put on your shot to score. Practise shooting from close in at first and

The Set Shot

1 With the foot on his shooting side slightly ahead, the shooter places his shooting hand on the back of and slightly under the ball with his fingers spread. He brings the ball up to just above head height with his non-shooting hand on the ball's side to steady it.

2 With his eyes on the basket throughout, the shooter bends his knees slightly. He then straightens from the legs up with his body and, finally, his shooting arm following.

3 The non-shooting hand lets go of the ball just before release. The wrist on the shooting hand, which has been bent back, snaps forward as the ball is released from the fingers. The shooter aims for a smooth follow-through with his arm pointing towards the target.

The Jump Shot

1 *From the set shot starting position but with the knees bent more, the player brings the ball up to around head height and jumps straight upwards. The fingers of the shooting hand point upwards with the non-shooting hand on the side of the ball.*

2 *The player releases the ball at the top of his jump sending it upwards. The ball is released with a flick of the wrists and fingers and the follow-through aims towards the target.*

then gradually work your way further out and from all different angles around the basket. Ask your coach to watch you in action and help you to remedy any faults.

Other Shots

Many spectacular shots made by top players at the Olympics or in the NBA are beyond the abilities of younger players. The slam dunk (see page 6), for instance, relies on players having great height and enough spring to position their hands well above the

basket. But however 'cool' or acrobatic a shot attempt is, it is still worth the same number of points as a simpler shot. Look for the simple option when you can.

The Suns Rise

In a 1990 NBA game against the Denver Nuggets, the Phoenix Suns racked up an incredible 107 points in the first half alone, an NBA record.

Regaining Possession

When players in a team lose possession of the ball, their aim is to do two things. They must try to stop the other team scoring a basket and regain the ball without incurring a foul or violation.

Loose Ball and Interceptions

When the ball breaks loose, it can signal a battle for possession between players from both teams. Awareness and quick reactions can ensure that one player gets to the ball first and secures it for their team. Players also stay alert for deflections, fumbled passes which may see the ball go loose, and air shots which do not reach the basket or the backboard. They also stay on the look-out for chances to intercept a poor pass. Some passes are thrown weakly, poorly aimed or look obvious well in advance. An alert opponent can sometimes intercept the ball

Rebounding

1 As a shot goes up, the defender gets into an excellent rebounding position. She has pivoted to face the basket and is in front of an opponent. This is called boxing or blocking out.

2 As the ball rebounds, the defender tries to predict the ball's flight and times her jump upwards. Her eyes watch the ball continually.

3 The defender's arms stretch upwards and she aims to take the ball at the very top of her jump with both hands. As the defender falls, she pulls her arms down and in to gather the ball into her chest.

and, with the other team on the attack and out of position, can launch a quick counter-attack.

Rebounding

A rebound is when a shot is attempted and the ball bounces back off the hoop or the backboard. It is important for attackers and defenders at all levels to be on the look-out for a rebound. In fact, beginners who master good rebounding will gain the ball many times in a game as many shots miss the basket but hit the backboard. Players have to predict where the ball is likely to bounce to when it rebounds, and move into a good position as early as possible. Whilst players are not allowed to push or barge their opponents, they can use their body as a shield.

The Next Move

With the rebound secure, players need to act quickly as they land. If on the attack, they may be able to send away another shot before defenders can react. Alternatively, they may look for a pass out of the key to a team-mate standing free in space. If a defender secures a rebound under their own basket, their first thought should be safety. They usually look for a safe pass to a team-mate in space, often out near the sideline. This is called an outlet pass.

Manu Ginobili rises high to reclaim the ball after a rebound.

Manu Ginobili

Date of birth: July 28th, 1977

Nationality: Argentinian

Height: 1.96m

Weight: 95kg

The Euroleague's most valuable player for two seasons in a row, when he played for Italian side Kinder Bologna, Manu Ginobili joined the San Antonio Spurs in 2002. He has won three NBA championships with the Spurs, most recently in 2007. A powerful presence under the basket, he scored 48 points in a single NBA game in 2005. A year earlier, he was voted the most valuable player at the 2004 Olympics where Argentina won the gold medal.

Defending

Defence in basketball relies on players performing individual tasks whilst also working as part of a team. If they lose the ball, players in the defending team aim to get back to their end of the court to guard their basket before their opponents reach it. One exception is the full court press where the defending team's players try to keep their opponents inside their own half for more than eight seconds to trigger a violation.

Zonal Marking

Marking is a vital part of team defence in basketball. A team's coach decides on which marking tactics to employ. Some teams may decide to mark zonally. This is where each player is responsible for a roughly circular area around the basket. These zones overlap slightly and often concentrate around the free throw line – this is a favoured place to shoot from.

One-on-One Marking

As its name suggests, one-on-one marking involves one defender closely marking one opponent. This may be the player with the ball or one of his or her four team-mates. When you are marking players without the ball, always try to deny them a chance to receive the ball by moving with them. At the same time, make sure you don't let them get free behind you so that they are

This defender is fouling his opponent by barging into him. Defenders should harass an opponent with the ball, trying to force a mistake and to stop the player sending away a good pass or shot, but not at an expense of a foul.

The defender (in blue) tries to track and keep close to his opponent dribbling the ball. He must be alert to the dribbler changing pace and direction to move away from him.

The Defensive Stance

1 This player is in the defensive stance. He faces his opponent with his arms out and hands spread trying to guard against the triple threat of passing, shooting and dribbling that their opponent poses. He is on his toes and alert for any move.

2 From the defensive stance, the defender has moved lower to cover an opponent's dribble. His arms are out and ready for any chance of stealing the ball should the dribbler lose control.

3 When a player stops dribbling he an only pivot, so a defender may stand a little closer to make passing or shooting difficult. Here the defender covers a shot by raising his arms.

closer to your basket than you. This takes great awareness of the court and your opponents as well as the ability to spot and cover fake moves by your opponent.

The Defensive Stance

The basic defensive stance when up against the player with the ball is similar to the triple threat stance, but players bend their knees more and crouch lower. From this position, players aim to move with quick shuffling steps on the balls of their feet as their opponent moves, always staying between the opposing player and the basket.

Selected Statistics

NBA Recent Champions

Year	Team	Most Valuable Player (MVP) Finals
2008-09	Cleveland	LeBron James
2006-07	San Antonio Spurs	Tony Parker
2005-06	Miami Heat	Dwayne Wade
2004-05	San Antonio Spurs	Tim Duncan
2003-04	Detroit Pistons	Chauncey Billups
2002-03	San Antonio Spurs	Tim Duncan
2001-02	Los Angeles Lakers	Shaquille O'Neal
2000-01	Los Angeles Lakers	Shaquille O'Neal
1999-00	Los Angeles Lakers	Shaquille O'Neal
1998-99	San Antonio Spurs	Tim Duncan
1997-98	Chicago Bulls	Michael Jordan
1996-97	Chicago Bulls	Michael Jordan
1995-96	Chicago Bulls	Michael Jordan
1994-95	Houston Rockets	Hakeem Olajuwon
1993-94	Houston Rockets	Hakeem Olajuwon
1992-93	Chicago Bulls	Michael Jordan
1991-92	Chicago Bulls	Michael Jordan
1990-91	Chicago Bulls	Michael Jordan
1989-90	Detroit Pistons	Isiah Thomas
1988-89	Detroit Pistons	Joe Dumars
1987-88	Los Angeles Lakers	James Worthy
1986-87	Los Angeles Lakers	Magic Johnson
1985-86	Boston Celtics	Larry Bird
1984-85	Los Angeles Lakers	Kareem Abdul-Jabbar
1983-84	Boston Celtics	Larry Bird
1982-83	Philadelphia 76ers	Moses Malone
1981-82	Los Angeles Lakers	Magic Johnson

Recent WNBA Champions

Year	Team
2009	Phoenix Mercury
2008	Detroit Shock
2007	Phoenix Mercury
2006	Detroit Shock
2005	Sacramento Monarchs
2004	Seattle Storm
2003	Detroit Shock
2002	Los Angeles Sparks
2001	Los Angeles Sparks
2000	Houston Comets

Recent FIBA World Champions

Year	Men	Women
2006	Spain	Australia
2002	Yugoslavia	USA
1998	Yugoslavia	USA
1994	USA	Brazil
1990	Yugoslavia	USA
1986	USA	USA

Recent European Basketball Championships Winners

Year	Men	Women
2009	Spain	France
2007	Russia	Russia
2005	Greece	Czech Republic
2003	Lithuania	Russia
2001	Yugoslavia	France
1999	Italy	Poland
1997	Yugoslavia	Lithuania
1995	Yugoslavia	Ukraine
1993	Germany	Spain
1991	Yugoslavia	Soviet Union
1989	Yugoslavia	Soviet Union
1987	Greece	Soviet Union
1985	Soviet Union	Soviet Union

Recent Olympic Champions

Year	Men	Women
2008	United States	United States
2004	Argentina	United States
2000	United States	United States
1996	United States	United States
1992	United States	Unified Team
1988	Soviet Union	United States
1984	United States	United States
1980	Yugoslavia	Soviet Union

Glossary

Assist A pass that leads directly to a scoring shot.

Back court The half of the court that a team is defending.

Back court violation When a team's players who are in their front court pass the ball back into the back court.

Blocking The illegal obstruction of an opposition player.

Cut A fast movement made by an attacker without the ball to find space.

Double Dribble A violation when a player dribbles the ball, catches it and then starts to dribble again.

Drive A fast, aggressive dribble towards the basket.

Field goal Any scoring shot other than a free throw.

Front court The end of the court that a team is attacking.

Key The marked out area around a basket in which attacking players are only allowed to stand for three seconds at a time.

Outlet pass A pass made by a defensive team receiving the ball, usually to a player who is free near the sideline.

Overtime An extra period of playing time to determine a winner if the scores are drawn.

Rebounding The skill of jumping and collecting the ball after it has bounced off the backboard or hoop.

Slam dunk A shot where the ball is thrust by the player's hand above the rim of the basket, down through the hoop to score.

Steal To win the ball from an opponent fairly.

Travelling A violation when a player takes too many steps after catching the ball.

Websites

www.nba.com

The official site of the NBA, this website is packed with statistics, results, player profiles and team news.

www.fiba.com

The website of the International Basketball Federation (FIBA), this is full of information about FIBA's junior and senior competitions.

www.eurobasket.com

This website has all the basketball news from Europe, searchable by country, as well as details of the Euro League and European Championships.

www.iwbf.org

The official website of the International Wheelchair Basketball Federation, packed with news stories, links and full rules for the game.

www.bbl.org.uk

The homepage of the British Basketball League has facts, stats and details of games to watch.

www.basketball.net.au

A website for fans of Australian basketball, with information on men's, women's and junior teams and competitions.

Note to parents and teachers: every effort has been made by the Publishers to ensure that these websites are suitable for children, that they are of the highest educational value, and that they contain no inappropriate or offensive material. However, because of the nature of the Internet, it is impossible to guarantee that the contents of these sites will not be altered. We strongly advise that Internet access is supervised by a responsible adult.

Index